The Kid
That Didn't Fit In

Written & Illustrated

By

Marla Harrison

It was the night before Christmas on a farm in South Georgia. Everything was quiet at the farm UNTIL a baby goat named Eve was born.

Eve's mother was unable to take care of her. The other goats in the herd were much bigger than Eve and some of them were mean to her! Eve was the kid that didn't fit in!

Eve was desperate! She needed a family to love her and take care of her! First, she had to find a way to escape the goat pen and herd!

Eve planned her escape! If she could somehow make it to the top of the hay, she could jump over the fence! Eve was very good at jumping!

Eve was brave and gave it a try! She climbed to the top of the hay, took a giant leap over the fence and landed safely outside the goat pen!

Now Eve could search for a new family!

Eve set out to explore the farm in hopes of finding a family she could call her own!

Eve found her way inside the pasture next to the goat pen and met a horse named Patches.

Patches introduced Eve to his family! Eve wondered if they could be her family too! But the farmer heard all the ruckus in the pasture and returned Eve to the goat pen!

The next morning, Eve knew she had to try again! She escaped the goat pen and visited Patches' family again. Then Eve went exploring the farm further! She needed to find a family!

Eve made it all the way to the farmer's house! The farmer's family took Eve inside and fed her and gave Eve lots of love! Later, the farmer returned Eve to the goat pen for the night.

The very next morning, Eve escaped the goat pen again and waited for the farmer's family outside on their porch!

The farmer and his family let Eve come inside! They fed her and gave her more LOVE! Then Eve knew she had found her family!

Eve was grateful to the farmer's family
for taking her in when she needed it
most! Eve wanted to thank the farmer's
family for taking such good care of her!

Eve helped on the farm, any way she could! She pulled all the weeds in the flower beds and garden. Eve loved eating the weeds!

Eve chewed on the grass so the farmer would not have to mow the lawn!

Eve helped the farmer feed all the animals on the farm, even the goats. The farmer's family was grateful for Eve's help around the farm!

Eve was so much help on the farm, the farmer decided to let Eve ride to his flower shop to help there too!

Eve loved going to the farmer's flower shop! There were so many weeds for her to munch on!! Eve loved helping the farmer and her new family!

Eve never had to escape the farm again!
She had finally found her herd!

Eve, the farmer's family, and farm animals all lived happily as ever as one big family!

Eve's Photo Gallery

Eve on Christmas 2023

Feedings with Eve

Meeting Patches & family

Eve thinks she's one of the herd!

Eve is waiting on the farmer's porch.

Eve helping the farmer's wife feed the farm animals.

Eve begging to go for a ride!

Eve hanging out with the rooster and cats!

Eve helping at the flower nursery

Goat Selfies with the Author

My husband, Adam, with Eve

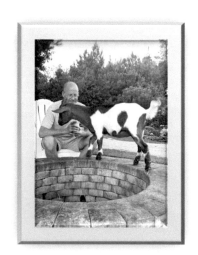

Author's Note

While writing this book I was reminded how blessed I am to have been born into such a wonderful, loving and accepting family but I was also reminded that not everyone is blessed as such! Family consists of the individuals you meet on your journey in life that pour love into you, whether it's the family you were born into or not. This book is dedicated to those still searching for their "herd" or "family" and acceptance! Be like Eve! Be brave, take a leap of faith and don't give up searching until you find those individuals that will love you and support you for who you are!

About the Author

Marla Harrison is a lifelong Georgia resident. She was born in Rome, Ga and graduated from Pepperell High School. She now resides in Douglas County with her husband, Adam. Marla and Adam have one daughter, a son-in-law and one granddaughter. Marla is the office manager for her family business in Tallapoosa, Ga and owns West Georgia Notary.

This is the fifth book Marla has written, illustrated and self-published. She also wrote *"When Sissy Met Lucy"*, *"Born To Sniff"*, *"Silly Sissy"*, and *"Sissy's Tales"*.

Made in the USA
Columbia, SC
22 November 2024

46203583R00018